Ages 5+

A
is for
AMAZING
Activity Book

Word Search
Find all the hidden words that are listed below. Words can be up, down, or across. Say the words out loud.

W E F W O L D B F Z U Z
A A D O R A B L E Z V A
D J G I P T M Y I V P C
V A N I M A T E D A S H
E I C B V X Q M F U A I
T P F V S B C H T M E M
U A D M I R A B L E C E
R D X P B X X M R N A R
O A W E S O M E Y T B W
U T K G E K L Q D I L B
S A M A Z I N G U C E P

AMAZING
AWESOME
ADORABLE
ADMIRABLE
ADVENTUROUS

AUTHENTIC
ANGELIC
ACHIEVER
AMICABLE
ANIMATED

Spot the Difference
Say the word out loud. Then find 5 differences between the pictures.

Imaginative

Dot to Dot
Say the word out loud. Connect the dots to complete the picture. Color it for fun.

Lovable

By Kelly Anderson
Illustrated by Salma Gull

Archway Publishing books may be ordered through booksellers or by contacting:

Archway Publishing
1663 Liberty Drive
Bloomington, IN 47403
www.archwaypublishing.com
844-669-3957

ISBN: 978-1-6657-2199-8 (sc)
ISBN: 978-1-6657-2198-1 (e)

Print information available on the last page.

Archway Publishing rev. date: 04/28/2022

ARCHWAY
PUBLISHING

This workbook belongs to:

Word Search

Find all the hidden words that are listed below. Words can be up, down, or across. Say the words out loud.

```
W  E  F  W  O  L  D  B  F  Z  U  Z
A  A  D  O  R  A  B  L  E  Z  V  A
D  J  G  I  P  T  M  Y  I  V  P  C
V  A  N  I  M  A  T  E  D  A  S  H
E  I  C  B  V  X  Q  M  F  U  A  I
N  A  N  G  E  L  I  C  S  T  M  E
T  P  F  V  S  B  C  H  T  H  I  V
U  A  D  M  I  R  A  B  L  E  C  E
R  D  X  P  B  X  X  M  R  N  A  R
O  A  W  E  S  O  M  E  Y  T  B  W
U  T  K  G  E  K  L  Q  D  I  L  B
S  A  M  A  Z  I  N  G  U  C  E  P
```

AMAZING	AUTHENTIC
AWESOME	ANGELIC
ADORABLE	ACHIEVER
ADMIRABLE	AMICABLE
ADVENTUROUS	ANIMATED

Heart Maze

Read the word. Find the way out of the heart and color the picture.

Angelic

FINISH

START

Scramble Words

Unscramble the words, they all start with the letter B.

FIUTALUBE

LTBRILNAI

RBVAE

EETENNOBVL

EGTBIDRHAE

EIMGOBNC

SDELBES

EREYZB

ULBYBB

BHTGRTAEIAKN

Dot to Dot

Say the word out loud. Connect the dots to complete the picture. Color it for fun!

Beautiful

Missing Letters

Fill in the missing letters to complete the words and write them in the blanks. Then say the words out loud.

Ch__r__i__g   _____

C_e_e___   _____

C___ ___l   _____

Co___ra___eo___s   _____

C___nsi___e___ate   _____

Co___ ___id___nt   _____

Cr___a___iv___   _____

Car___fu___   _____

C___n___id   _____

Ca___a___l__   _____

Clever	Cool	Courageous	Considerate	Confident
Creative	Careful	Candid	Capable	Charming

Coloring Picture

Say the word out loud. Color the picture for fun.

Charming

Make Sentences

Say the words out loud. Use them to make simple sentences.

Words	Sentences
1. Delightful	
2. Dazzling	
3. Decent	
4. Dependable	
5. Disciplined	
6. Dedicated	
7. Dynamic	
8. Devoted	
9. Dainty	
10. Determined	

Secret Words

Use the key below to reveal the secret words. Then say the words out loud.

1. __ __ __ __ __ __ __ __ __ __ __
   7   5   @   %   5   8   4   5   }   #   7

2. __ __ __ __ __ __ __
   7   #   {   2   *   #   7

3. __ __ __ __ __ __ __ __ __ __
   7   #   *   #   9   ?   5   }   #   7

4. __ __ __ __ __ __ __ __
   7   3   =   =   4   5   }   (

A	B	C	D	E	F	G
3	!	%	7	#	$	(

H	I	J	K	L	M	N
1	5	:	6	4	?	}

O	P	Q	R	S	T	U
2	8	0	9	@	*	)

V	W	X	Y	Z
{	/	;	+	=

Word Search

Find all the hidden words that are listed below. Words can be up, down, or across. Say the words out loud.

```
S  I  P  E  O  A  E  E  L  E  G  Q  N
L  N  X  A  G  L  N  X  C  W  E  E  W
J  U  B  S  S  H  T  T  P  J  C  X  P
R  W  E  Y  D  E  H  R  K  C  S  C  E
F  W  X  G  N  N  U  A  E  U  T  E  N
A  J  E  O  E  C  S  O  L  Y  A  L  D
Q  Y  M  I  A  H  I  R  E  Y  T  L  E
E  B  P  N  R  A  A  D  G  L  I  E  A
D  N  L  G  N  N  S  I  A  Z  C  N  R
Z  I  A  O  E  T  T  N  N  A  U  T  I
S  E  R  Y  S  I  I  A  T  H  H  Z  N
O  I  F  P  T  N  C  R  W  E  D  G  G
G  O  V  C  J  G  N  Y  F  I  Y  N  R
```

EXTRAORDINARY	EXCELLENT
ELEGANT	ENTHUSIASTIC
ENCHANTING	EASY GOING
ENDEARING	EARNEST
EXEMPLAR	ECSTATIC

Sudoku

Every row, column, and 2x2 block must contain the following words once. Read the words aloud.

1. Elegant   2. Ecstatic   3. Earnest   4. Excellent

Excellent	Ecstatic		
	Ernest		
		Elegant	

Practice the words with the beginning sound E.

_____

_____

_____

Write Synonyms

Say the words out loud. Write two synonyms for each word.

1. Fabulous

1. _____
2. _____

2. Friendly

1. _____
2. _____

3. Funny

1. _____
2. _____

4. Fantastic

1. _____
2. _____

5. Fascinating

1. _____
2. _____

6. Favored

1. _____
2. _____

7. Fearless

1. _____
2. _____

8. Famous

1. _____
2. _____

9. Flawless

1. _____
2. _____

10. Front-runner

1. _____
2. _____

Coloring Picture

Read the word. Color the picture for fun.

Friendly

Word Search

Find all the hidden words that are listed below. Words can be up, down, or across. Say the words out loud.

G E N U I N E X V D Z N
W G A L L A N T D G F H
Q M A Z B Q Z Y E R Q L
G U T S Y G Z Y B A C S
W X G E N I U S R C B N
G O O D N A T U R E D H
O C Z A O U I K X F O T
C T A G O R G E O U S Z
F G X A F D H F F L W I
D G I F T E D X F Y I L
C B X F C K G E N T L E
G E N E R O U S M R X P

GORGEOUS   GUTSY
GENEROUS   GOOD NATURED
GENIUS   GRACEFUL
GALLANT   GIFTED
GENUINE   GENTLE

Count and Write

Count the words and write the correct number in the box.
Say the words out loud.

Gifted   Genuine   Gentle   Genuine

Genius   Gifted

Genuine   Gutsy

Genuine

Gutsy   Gentle   Gifted

Gallant   Gutsy

Genuine

Gifted   Graceful

Genuine   Gifted

Gutsy

Gifted   Generous   Gutsy

Gallant

Gutsy

Gentle

Gutsy   Gentle   Generous

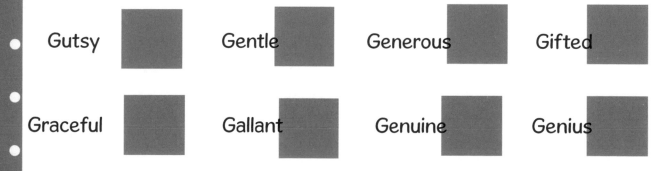

Gutsy ☐   Gentle ☐   Generous ☐   Gifted ☐

Graceful ☐   Gallant ☐   Genuine ☐   Genius ☐

Scramble Words

Unscramble the words, they all start with the letter H.

LVYEHAEN

BELMUH

FLELUPH

RROKNDWAGIH

MEHANODS

PYHPA

AEUBGHGL

ELHHATY

REHCOI

NHSOTE

Dot to Dot

Say the word out loud. Connect the dots to complete the picture.
Color it for fun!

Huggable

Missing Letters

Fill in the missing letters to complete the words and write them in the blanks. Then say the words out loud.

In___re___ib___e   _____

I___pr___ss___ve   _____

In___el___ig___nt   _____

Inn___ce___t   _____

Ima___in___ti___e   _____

I___s___ir___ng   _____

In___ui___iti___e   _____

I___oni___   _____

Ir___es___sti___le   _____

I___pi___h   _____

Innocent	Imaginative	Impressive	Inspiring	Iconic
Irresistible	Incredible	Intelligent	Inquisitive	Impish

Spot the Difference

Say the word out loud. Then find 5 differences between the pictures.

Imaginative

Make Sentences

Say the words out loud. Use them to make simple sentences.

Words	Sentences
1. Joyful	
2. Judicious	
3. Jubilant	
4. Jaunty	
5. Jovial	
6. Jolly	
7. Jocular	
8. Jazzy	
9. Jeweled	
10. Jaw-dropping	

Square Maze

Say the word out loud. Help the guitarist find the notes.

Jazzy

Word Search

Find all the hidden words that are listed below. Words can be up, down, or across. Say the words out loud.

H	P	H	B	G	M	J	T	K	R	G	V	N
K	I	N	D	R	E	D	U	N	K	I	K	H
Q	K	G	A	K	T	K	Z	O	H	Z	K	S
H	Y	S	O	I	E	E	M	W	K	R	I	U
K	T	M	U	N	K	N	N	L	R	K	N	K
I	N	G	R	E	U	S	Y	E	V	N	D	K
T	I	A	T	T	D	P	P	D	B	I	H	E
T	N	Q	G	I	O	E	E	G	B	G	E	M
E	O	A	S	C	S	C	E	E	C	H	A	P
N	A	W	B	Q	T	K	K	A	U	T	R	T
I	Y	V	A	Z	J	L	E	B	W	L	T	Z
S	L	X	I	U	W	E	E	L	R	Y	E	B
H	M	U	M	D	R	H	N	E	O	G	D	P

KITTENISH

KENSPECKLE

KNIGHTLY

KUDOS

KINDRED

KEEN

KNOWLEDGEABLE

KINETIC

KEMPT

KIND-HEARTED

Sudoku

Every row, column, and 2x2 block must contain the following words once. Read the words aloud.

1. Keen   2. Kinetic   3. Kempt   4. Kudos

Kinetic			
	Keen		
			Kempt
Kempt			Kudos

Practice the words with the beginning sound K.

_____

_____

_____

_____

Write Synonyms

Say the words out loud. Write two synonyms for each word.

1. Lovely

1. _____
2. _____

2. Lovable

1. _____
2. _____

3. Likable

1. _____
2. _____

4. Loyal

1. _____
2. _____

5. Lively

1. _____
2. _____

6. Laudable

1. _____
2. _____

7. Legendary

1. _____
2. _____

8. Lionhearted

1. _____
2. _____

9. Lifesaver

1. _____
2. _____

10. Leader

1. _____
2. _____

Dot to Dot

Say the word out loud. Connect the dots to complete the picture. Color it for fun.

Lovable

Word Search

Find all the hidden words that are listed below. Words can be up, down, or across. Say the words out loud.

```
M  A  R  V  E  L  O  U  S  O  Y  G
M  A  G  N  I  F  I  C  E  N  T  Q
M  O  T  I  V  A  T  E  D  M  E  M
J  M  E  L  L  O  W  A  L  E  H  E
G  L  T  P  S  A  K  X  E  T  W  G
H  G  E  T  N  D  K  M  E  I  N  A
M  E  R  R  Y  Z  V  Z  F  C  L  S
M  E  L  O  D  I  C  M  W  U  M  T
M  A  G  I  C  A  L  W  K  L  B  A
G  Y  X  H  I  E  F  B  Z  O  M  R
M  A  G  N  A  N  I  M  O  U  S  B
D  M  A  M  L  Q  F  Y  D  S  B  Y
```

MARVELOUS   MAGNANIMOUS
MAGNIFICENT   MAGICAL
MOTIVATED   MEGA STAR
METICULOUS   MERRY
MELLOW   MELODIC

Spot the Difference

Say the word out loud. Then find 10 differences between the pictures.

Marvelous

Scramble Words

Unscramble the words, they all start with the letter N.

EBATNOL

HENGOYLIBR

NAELBCETOI

ATNARLU

LEMBIN

OLBNE

ONTROETWYH

OLVEN

ETRRUNUR

ITFYN

Count and Write

Count the words and write the correct number in the box. Say the words out loud.

Natural
Natural
Notable
Notable
Notable
Noble
Novel
Noble
Nifty
Noble
Notable
Novel
Natural
Notable
Nifty
Notable
Novel
Novel
Noble
Novel
Notable
Notable
Nimble
Novel
Natural
Notable
Noble
Natural
Natural
Novel
Natural
Nimble
Nifty
Notable
Notable
Novel
Natural
Noble
Nimble

Notable ▢

Noble ▢

Natural ▢

Nifty ▢

Novel ▢

Nimble ▢

Missing Letters

Fill in the missing letters to complete the words and write them in the blanks. Then say the words out loud.

Ou___st___n___ing _____

O___se___van _____

Org___ni___e _____

O___je___t___ve _____

Op___im___s___ic _____

O___ig___n___l _____

Ob___di___n___ _____

O___t___hi___e _____

O___a___or _____

Orn___m___nta___ _____

Secret Words

Use the key below to reveal the secret words. Then say the words out loud.

1. ___ ___ ___ ___ ___ ___ ___ ___ ___ ___ ___
   2   )   *   @   *   3   }   7   5   }   (

2. ___ ___ ___ ___ ___ ___ ___ ___ ___ ___
   2   8   *   5   ?   5   @   *   5   %

3. ___ ___ ___ ___ ___ ___ ___ ___ ___ ___
   2   9   }   3   ?   #   }   *   3   4

4. ___ ___ ___ ___ ___ ___ ___ ___
   2   !   #   7   5   #   }   *

A	B	C	D	E	F	G
3	!	%	7	#	$	(
H	I	J	K	L	M	N
1	5	:	6	4	?	}
O	P	Q	R	S	T	U
2	8	0	9	@	*	)
	V	W	X	Y	Z	
	{	/	;	+	=	

Make Sentences

Say the words out loud. Use them to make simple sentences.

Words	Sentences
1. Phenomenal	
2. Philanthropic	
3. Pretty	
4. Perfect	
5. Priceless	
6. Polite	
7. Personable	
8. Popular	
9. Perky	
10. Peaceful	

Spot the Difference

Say the word out loud. Then find 7 differences between the pictures.

Peaceful

Word Search

Find all the hidden words that are listed below. Words can be up, down, or across. Say the words out loud.

```
W  Q  A  U  G  D  B  M  C  H  S  B  E  Q
Q  U  I  E  S  C  E  N  T  Q  W  Q  Q  U
U  A  T  R  C  N  O  I  O  U  K  U  U  O
I  D  L  T  X  Y  M  S  V  I  O  W  Q  T
C  Y  Q  R  U  L  U  L  E  C  L  W  U  A
K  K  A  W  J  V  B  R  B  K  W  T  A  B
W  P  Y  F  Q  U  I  X  O  T  I  C  L  L
I  P  V  Y  T  U  M  O  S  H  K  D  I  E
T  C  Y  U  L  S  T  Y  J  I  M  I  T  P
T  V  I  M  W  Q  U  E  E  N  L  Y  Y  N
E  N  J  B  A  P  Y  I  A  K  I  W  Q  T
D  F  X  K  Z  Q  U  A  L  I  F  I  E  D
Q  U  I  N  T  E  S  S  E  N  T  I  A  L
C  S  N  Q  U  I  R  K  Y  G  L  X  B  C
```

QUEENLY	QUIESCENT
QUIRKY	QUICK-WITTED
QUICK-THINKING	QUALITY
QUALIFIED	QUIXOTIC
QUINTESSENTIAL	QUOTABLE

Coloring Picture

Read the word. Color the picture for fun.

Quirky

Write Synonyms

Say the words out loud. Write two synonyms for each word.

1. Remarkable

1. _____
2. _____

2. Responsible

1. _____
2. _____

3. Radiant

1. _____
2. _____

4. Respectful

1. _____
2. _____

5. Reliable

1. _____
2. _____

6. Refreshing

1. _____
2. _____

7. Resourceful

1. _____
2. _____

8. Resilient

1. _____
2. _____

9. Regal

1. _____
2. _____

10. Realistic

1. _____
2. _____

Secret Words

Use the key below to reveal the secret words. Then say the words out loud.

1. ___ ___ ___ ___ ___ ___ ___ ___ ___ ___

   9   #   @   8   #   %   * $)   4

2. ___ ___ ___ ___ ___ ___ ___ ___ ___ ___

   9   #   ?   9   6   3   3   !   4   #

3. ___ ___ ___ ___ ___ ___ ___ ___ ___

   9   #   @   5   4   5   #   }   *

4. ___ ___ ___ ___ ___ ___ ___ ___ ___

   9   #   3   4   5   @   *   5   %

A	B	C	D	E	F	G
3	!	%	7	#	$	(
H	I	J	K	L	M	N
1	5	:	6	4	?	}
O	P	Q	R	S	T	U
2	8	0	9	@	*	)
	V	W	X	Y	Z	
	{	/	;	+	=	

Word Search

Find all the hidden words that are listed below. Words can be up, down, or across. Say the words out loud.

```
S  S  O  C  I  A  B  L  E  S  S  F
E  C  Q  R  N  F  S  F  M  P  S  V
N  A  T  A  S  Z  P  J  S  E  T  Y
S  U  P  E  R  B  E  M  E  C  U  O
A  S  I  F  V  S  C  S  R  I  N  P
T  W  I  S  V  E  T  A  E  A  N  C
I  J  P  I  S  N  A  V  N  L  I  L
O  M  D  N  D  S  C  V  E  C  N  N
N  G  L  C  Q  I  U  Y  D  U  G  N
A  O  G  E  F  B  L  T  H  O  A  S
L  E  W  R  D  L  A  I  W  S  E  L
V  E  P  E  F  E  R  J  K  F  C  G
```

SPECTACULAR	SAVVY
STUNNING	SERENE
SUPERB	SOCIABLE
SPECIAL	SENSIBLE
SENSATIONAL	SINCERE

Spot the Difference

Say the word out loud. Then find 7 differences between the pictures.

Spectacular

Scramble Words

Unscramble the words, they all start with the letter T.

TTOCPONH

LTHGFHUOTU

EERSOUNDMT

ERARTESU

NTLADTEE

MARETAYEPL

FCRITEIR

LTFTUCA

HBTAEAELC

UTTHSTRRWOY

Sudoku

Every row, column, and 2x2 block must contain the following words once. Read the words aloud.

1. Terrific   2. Tactful   3. Treasure   4. Talented

		Tactful	Terrific
	Treasure		Talented

Write the words that start from the letter T.

_____

_____

_____

_____

Missing Letters

Fill in the missing letters to complete the words and write them in the blanks. Then say the words out loud.

Un___eli___va___le _____

U___b___a___ _____

Ul___im___t___ _____

U___s___a___ding _____

Un___on___iti nal _____

U___i___ue _____

Un___to___pa___le _____

U___ef___l _____

Up___if___ _____

U___der___ta___ding _____

Coloring Picture

Read the word. Color the picture for fun.

Upbeat

Make Sentences

Say the words out loud. Use them to make simple sentences.

Words	Sentences
1. Vivacious	
2. Valuable	
3. Virtuous	
4. Vibrant	
5. Vogue	
6. Valiant	
7. Validated	
8. Victorious	
9. Veteran	
10. Vital	

Dot to Dot

Say the word out loud. Connect the dots to complete the picture. Color it for fun!

Victorious

Word Search

Find all the hidden words that are listed below. Words can be up, down, or across. Say the words out loud.

```
C  W  W  O  N  D  E  R  F  U  L  U  G
C  G  H  Q  Q  W  W  I  L  L  I  N  G
B  X  I  O  N  O  E  G  W  W  D  R  W
P  Q  M  V  D  R  K  A  A  H  G  Q  I
L  W  S  G  U  T  N  E  R  O  C  W  T
U  I  I  Y  L  H  K  F  M  L  A  I  T
Y  N  C  B  F  Y  B  O  H  E  B  N  Y
Y  S  A  D  N  W  K  L  E  S  N  N  Z
R  O  L  S  R  M  I  D  A  O  M  E  T
J  M  Y  T  R  B  K  H  R  M  K  R  U
N  E  X  X  A  W  V  Q  T  E  D  E  T
W  E  L  L  M  A  N  N  E  R  E  D  L
X  Z  C  W  F  D  C  Q  D  F  W  Y  C
```

WONDERFUL

WITTY

WELL MANNERED

WORTHY

WARM HEARTED

WINNER

WHIMSICAL

WINSOME

WILLING

WHOLESOME

Spot the Difference

Say the word out loud. Then find 7 differences between the pictures.

Wonderful

Word Search

Find all the hidden words that are listed below. Words can be up, down, or across. Say the words out loud.

```
X  U  A  P  D  U  D  R  E  Y  I  X
X  A  N  T  H  I  C  H  X  Q  A  N
Y  O  X  A  N  O  L  A  L  I  A  K
L  D  J  U  X  R  R  W  Q  H  R  X
O  C  D  V  E  W  M  L  V  V  A  E
G  Z  R  N  W  X  F  U  P  R  J  N
R  X  C  K  K  F  A  C  I  Z  R  I
A  X  X  A  N  A  G  O  G  U  E  A
P  P  Q  V  A  C  K  A  J  D  N  L
H  E  C  V  A  T  Q  V  V  F  Z  D
I  R  W  J  D  O  X  E  N  A  S  X
C  K  E  W  A  R  T  F  X  O  Q  N
```

XENIAL   XANAGOGUE
XPER   XANOLALIA
XFACTOR   XYLOGRAPHIC
XENAS   XANTHIC

Sudoku

Every row, column, and 3x3 block must contain the following words once. Read the words aloud.

1. Xenial   2. Xper   3. X-factor

4. Xenas   5. Xanthic   6. Xanolalia

		Xenas			Xanolalia
		X-factor			Xenas
Xenas			Xenial		
			Xanolalia		
	Xenas		X-factor		

Count and Write

Count the words and write the correct number in the box.
Say the words out loud.

Yummy   Yuppie   Younker   Yern

Yern   Yern   Yock

Yuppue   Younker   Younker   Yuppie

Youthful   Younker

Yern   Yuppie   Yern

Yummy   Yock   Yern

Yock   Yuppie   Younker   Younker   Yummy

Yern   Yuppie   Youthful

Yuppie   Younker   Yuppie   Younker

Yummy

Yock   Yock

Yock   Yern   Yuppie   Yern

Yern   Yern   Yern

Yern   Yock   Yuppue

Yummy   Younker   Youthful

Coloring Picture

Read the word. Color the picture for fun.

Yummy

Missing Letters

Fill in the missing letters to complete the words and write them in the blanks. Then say the words out loud.

Ze___t___   _____

Z___n___   _____

Z___p___y   _____

Za___z___   _____

Ze___   _____

Z___n___y   _____

Z___a___ou___   _____

Zi___ ___y   _____

Z___l___io___   _____

Z___o___y   _____

Sudoku

Every row, column, and 3x3 block must contain the following words once. Read the words aloud.

1. Zen   2. Zany   3. Zippy

4. Zesty   5. Zingy   6. Zillion

			Zippy	Zen	
	Zen			Zany	
	Zesty				
		Zingy			
	Zillion	Zen	Zesty		

Printed in the United States
by Baker & Taylor Publisher Services